MARTIN LUTHER KING JR.

THIS EDITION
Produced for DK by WonderLab Group LLC
Jennifer Emmett, Erica Green, Kate Hale, *Founders*

Editor Maya Myers; **Photography Editor** Nicole DiMella; **Managing Editor** Rachel Houghton;
Designers Project Design Company; **Researcher** Michelle Harris; **Copy Editor** Lori Merritt; **Indexer** Connie Binder;
Proofreader Susan K. Hom; **Series Reading Specialist** Dr. Jennifer Albro; **Sensitivity Reader** Ebonye Gussine Wilkins

First American Edition, 2025
Published in the United States by DK Publishing, a division of Penguin Random House LLC
1745 Broadway, 20th Floor, New York, NY 10019

Copyright © 2025 Dorling Kindersley Limited
24 25 26 27 10 9 8 7 6 5 4 3 2 1
001–345877–May/2025

All rights reserved.
Without limiting the rights under the copyright reserved above, no part of this publication may be reproduced, stored in or introduced into a retrieval system, or transmitted, in any form, or by any means (electronic, mechanical, photocopying, recording, or otherwise), without the prior written permission of the copyright owner.
Published in Great Britain by Dorling Kindersley Limited

A catalog record for this book is available from the Library of Congress.
HC ISBN: 978-0-5939-6635-8
PB ISBN: 978-0-5939-6634-1

DK books are available at special discounts when purchased in bulk for sales promotions, premiums, fund-raising, or educational use.
For details, contact:
DK Publishing Special Markets, 1745 Broadway, 20th Floor, New York, NY 10019
SpecialSales@dk.com

Printed and bound in China
Super Readers Lexile® levels 800L to 1010L
Lexile® is the registered trademark of MetaMetrics, Inc. Copyright © 2024 MetaMetrics, Inc. All rights reserved.

The publisher would like to thank the following for their kind permission to reproduce their images:
a=above; c=center; b=below; l=left; r=right; t=top; b/g=background
Adobe Stock: davidevison 31tr; **Alamy Stock Photo:** AP Photo / Charles Kelly 51t, Archivio GBB 6b, Associated Press 36tl, Arpad Benedek 54tl, Robert K. Chin - Storefronts 15t, dpa picture alliance / CNP / Chris Kleponis 57cl, Everett Collection Historical 25cr, Everett Collection Historical / Ron Harvey 12, Everett Collection Inc 25tl, Geopix 4-5, Heritage Image Partnership Ltd 46br, IanDagnall Computing 57br, 61bl, Jeffrey Isaac Greenberg 12+ 55tr, MediaPunch / Benjamin E. "Gene" Forte - CNP 58tl, PA Images 15cra, Pictorial Press Ltd 28t, PictureLux / The Hollywood Archive 20, Mark Scheuern 13b, Science History Images 11bl; **Morehouse College:** 14b; **Dreamstime.com:** Steve Allen 40tl, Avmedved 45cr, F11photo 50b, Konstik 43tr, Kooslin 14tl, QualitDesign 23 (flag), Rogerothornhill 56-57, David M. Schrader 13clb, Joe Sohm 13tr, Leonid Sorokin 49b; **Getty Images:** Afro Newspaper / Gado 57cbr, Bettmann 3, 10tl, 26br, 31l, 35tl, 47, 57tr, 57cra, 58cl, 58b, Morton Broffman 44-45, 61cr, Chicago History Museum 1, The Chronicle Collection / Don Cravens 18bl, 19, 21bl, 60bl, Corbis Historical / David Pollack 35cr, Corbis Premium Historical / Flip Schulke Archives 6tl, CQ-Roll Call, Inc. / Chris Maddaloni 56b, Don Cravens 16-17b, Daily Express / Archive Photos / Hulton Archive 60br, Gado 27tr, Ron Galella 55cr, Houston Chronicle / Hearst Newspapers / Jon Shapley 17cr, Robin Marchant 59tr, Michael Ochs Archives 16tl, 26-27t, 61cl, Michael Ochs Archives / Steve Wasserman 44tl, New York Daily News Archive / Tony Pescatore 56c, Robert Abbott Sengstacke 52-53b, Rolls Press / Popperfoto 52tl, The Chronicle Collection / Cynthia Johnson 54-55, Tony Tomsic 41t, TPLP 22, 42, Tony Vaccaro 12cla; **Getty Images / iStock:** gmast3r 60-61, SeanPavonePhoto 21tr; **IMAGN:** Vernon Matthews / The Commercial Appeal via USA TODAY via Imagn Content Services, LLC 48; **LBJ Library:** White House Photo Office / Cecil Stoughton 33tr, 61tc, White House Photo Office Yoichi Okamoto 32-33; **Library of Congress, Washington, D.C.:** LC-DIG-fsa-8a26761 / Lee, Russell, 1903-1986 10, LC-DIG-pga-06132 9tr, LC-DIG-ppmsc-01270 / Trikosko, Marion S, photographer 57fbr, LC-USF34-040837-D / Delano, Jack, photographer 38, LC-USZ6-1847 / Trikosko, Marion S, photographer 41bl, LC-USZ62-27663 111l, LC-USZ62-67819 / O'Sullivan, Timothy H 8-9t; **The Metropolitan Museum of Art:** Gift of Robert Lehman, 1955 7tr; **National Archives:** 30bl; **Shutterstock.com:** Eric Glenn 7crb, HannaChu 7l; **U.S. government works:** Oliver Contreras 29tr, FBI media 26tl

Cover images: *Front:* **Getty Images:** Bettmann, Hulton Archive (background);
Back: **Getty Images:** Hulton Archive / Heritage Images cl, Hulton Archive / Timelapse Library Ltd. / Tony Evans cra

www.dk.com

This book was made with Forest Stewardship Council™ certified paper – one small step in DK's commitment to a sustainable future.
Learn more at www.dk.com/uk/information/sustainability

Publisher's note: This book uses terms for Black Americans as appropriate to modern and historical contexts. Historical terms are defined in the glossary.

Level 4

MARTIN LUTHER KING JR.

Angela Bull and Matt Myers

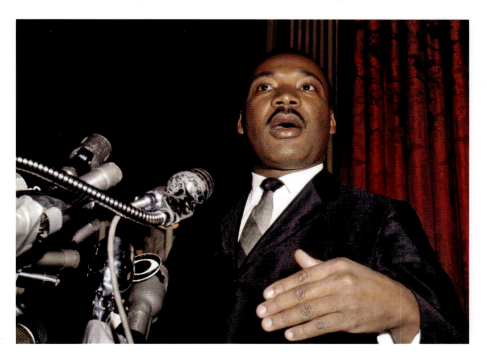

CONTENTS

6	A Boy Who Would Lead
14	The Peaceful Fight Begins
24	The National Stage
30	I Have a Dream
40	The Other Struggle
46	Murder in Memphis
52	A Powerful Legacy

King at the March on Washington, August 28, 1963

56	*We* Shall Overcome
58	Coretta's Journey
60	A Nonviolent Revolution
62	Glossary
63	Index
64	Quiz

Martin Luther King Sr.

Minister
Different faiths have different names for a religious leader who serves a community of believers. Some titles include minister, pastor, priest, imam, and rabbi.

A BOY WHO WOULD LEAD

The young boy looked at himself in the mirror and smiled. He had a new name.

He had been Michael King. But this morning, his father, the minister of his family's church, had announced the boy's new name to the whole congregation. He was now Martin Luther King Junior. He was called Junior (Jr. for short) because his father's name was also Martin Luther King.

It was a name the whole world would come to know.

Martin the Protester

Both Martin and his father were named in honor of German monk Martin Luther (1483–1546). Luther thought religion had become too complicated and oppressive. His protests against these changes marked the beginning of the Protestant church.

Plaque in front of Martin's childhood home in Atlanta, Georgia

Enslaved people on a South Carolina plantation, 1862

Big Business
Millions of Black people were captured in Africa, chained, and sent on ships to the Americas. In the US, Africans were sold in slave markets. One market was located within sight of the White House.

Martin was born in Atlanta, Georgia, on January 15, 1929. Back then, Black people were expected to follow countless rules that kept them from being truly free. This was especially true in the American South, where slavery had been legal just 64 years earlier.

Martin's great-grandparents had been enslaved in Georgia. They were forced to work all their lives for no pay.

The Civil War (1861–1865) While slavery was illegal in the northern states, southern states wanted it to continue. These states formed a new country called the Confederacy. The two sides went to war, and it's estimated that more than 700,000 soldiers died.

They had no rights. They could be bought and sold, just like horses.

Slavery ended after the Civil War. Yet even when Martin was growing up, segregation laws (also known as Jim Crow laws) kept Black people from being free. "Whites only" signs banned Black people from shops, restaurants, and even churches.

9

Forced Separation
Segregation is forcibly separating people by their race. The separation can be total, such as when the US forced Indigenous Americans to live on reservations. It can also be limited to certain situations, such as when Black and white children couldn't attend the same schools.

In addition to schools and restaurants, bathrooms and even drinking fountains were segregated.

When Martin was little, his best friend was white. Their different skin colors meant they couldn't go to the same school. They couldn't play in the same parks, swim in the same pools, or even drink from the same water fountains.

Jesse Owens

The older Martin got, the fewer choices he saw for his future. For a Black person in the US, becoming a leader in business or government was next to impossible. Martin wanted to make his mark in the world, but how? Should he be a pastor, like his father? Or an athlete? He was small but strong. After all, Jesse Owens and Joe Louis were world champions, and they were Black.

Jesse Owens
When Germany's racist dictator Adolf Hitler hosted the 1936 Olympics in Berlin, the last thing he wanted was Jewish or Black athletes to compete. American Jesse Owens not only competed, but won four gold medals.

Joe Louis
Heavyweight champion of the world for almost 12 years, American Joe Louis kept the title longer than any other boxer in history. He also enraged Hitler, beating the "unbeatable" German champion Max Schmeling in 1938. Yet Louis also endured hateful racism in the US.

Back of the Bus
Many cities required Black riders to take the last seats at the back of the bus so white riders wouldn't have to walk past them. And if the front seats filled up, whites could take any Black person's seat they wanted—even if the person was sitting there first.

One thing Martin had going for him was his way with words. He had a strong voice, and his passion was inspiring. When he was 15, he gave a speech called "The Negro and the Constitution" in a statewide public speaking contest. In the speech, he compared the high ideals of the United States to the reality of the inequality its people faced.

Martin and his teacher rode a bus to the contest. On the way, when the bus filled up, Martin was told to give up his seat to a white man. At first, he refused, but his teacher reminded him of the rule: "Whites before blacks." Martin had to stand in the back of the bus for several hours.

Martin never forgot that. "It was the angriest I have ever been in my life," he said, years later.

> "We cannot have a nation orderly and sound with one group so ground down and thwarted that it is almost forced into unsocial attitudes and crime."
>
> —from King's contest speech

At the Martin Luther King Jr. Kingdom Day Parade in Los Angeles, California, 2015

Changing Language
The word Negro is now considered outdated and can be considered offensive. But it was once a respectful term, used by Black and white people alike. Language is always changing. What is considered correct today may not be so in the future.

Replica of a 1950s Montgomery bus

THE PEACEFUL FIGHT BEGINS

Martin had a strong Christian faith, so he eventually decided to use his gift for public speaking as a Baptist minister. After graduating from Morehouse College in 1948, he went on to Crozer Theological Seminary to study religion. He finished at the top of his class and spoke at his graduation. Martin was a minister now, but he wanted to know more. In 1951, he entered Boston University, where he earned a doctorate in theology. This made his name even longer—the Reverend Dr. Martin Luther King Jr.

A Different Kind of Doctor
A doctorate degree makes someone a doctor of philosophy (or PhD). They study certain kinds of ideas or academic subjects.

King graduating from Morehouse College, 1948

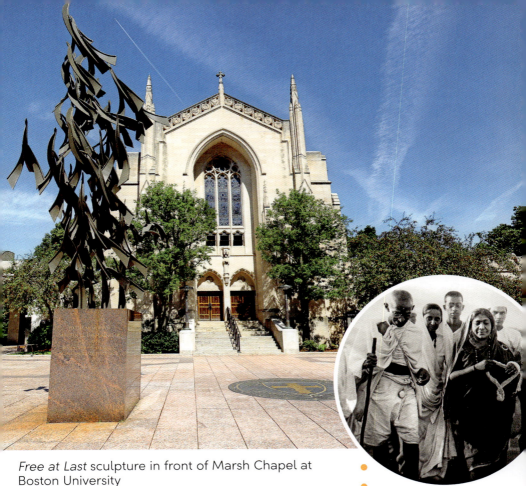

Free at Last sculpture in front of Marsh Chapel at Boston University

In Boston, Martin met Coretta Scott, who was studying music. She was also passionate about equal rights. They were both impressed with the Indian leader Mahatma Gandhi, who had used nonviolent resistance to overturn centuries of white rule in India. Could this be a way to get equal rights for Black Americans?

Nonviolent Resistance
Leaders like King and Gandhi put themselves in danger when it was necessary to make change happen. King called the strategy "a courageous confrontation of evil by the power of love."

First Date
Martin was impressed by Coretta from the start. She was already a more experienced activist, and on their first date, they debated about different types of government.

In 1953, Martin and Coretta got married. They moved to Montgomery, Alabama, where Martin became the minister of a church. His sermons linked faith with working for equality.

Montgomery had a long history of racism. A whole web of laws was in place to restrict the movements and opportunities of Black people. For years, the Women's Political Council and the NAACP had been demanding change, without success.

King speaking to organizers of the bus boycott in January 1956

But in December 1955, when NAACP worker Rosa Parks was jailed for calmly refusing to give up her bus seat to a white person, the Black community seized the moment to mobilize and fight back.

King was ready to help. He'd been ready ever since hearing the rule, "Whites before blacks."

Rosa Parks on a Montgomery bus

NAACP
The National Association for the Advancement of Colored People was created in 1909. Its ongoing goal is to fight discrimination through legal means.

17

Boycott
In 1880, poor Irish farmers protested their harsh conditions by refusing to pay rent to Charles Boycott. Boycott's name came to stand for any refusal to deal with unfair people or businesses.

The plan was to boycott the bus company. Since 75 percent of bus riders were Black, if they quit paying to ride the buses, it would mean a huge loss of income for the bus company and the city. This boycott was a peaceful way to protest, and King got behind it in a big way.

Black people stopped riding buses. Others with cars volunteered to drive those who had no other way to get around. King was excited. The nonviolent protest seemed to be working.

The peaceful boycott went on for more than a year. King's passion was answered by hate mail and death threats. A bomb exploded in his house. No one was hurt, but the racist message was clear: Stop making trouble.

King at the end of the bus boycott, December 1956

18

"It is more honorable to walk in dignity than ride in humiliation."

—Martin Luther King Jr.

People walking to work in Montgomery, February 1956

King was arrested a total of 29 times for his protests.

20

The city of Montgomery used any excuse to get King behind bars. First, he was arrested for conspiracy. Then, the city invented a new law to stop car owners from giving rides to other people. King had helped organize the carpooling system, so he was arrested again. He had to go to court for breaking this new law.

But the trial had hardly begun when news came that the Supreme Court had declared bus segregation to be unconstitutional. The Montgomery bus boycott had changed history.

Supreme Court
The Supreme Court is the highest court in the nation. Nine judges make the final decision on legal cases, based on their interpretation of the Constitution.

The Constitution
In 1787, a list of laws was written to protect the rights of US citizens, though for many years it mostly protected the rights of white men. Any law or action that is found to go against the Constitution is considered unconstitutional.

21

What If?
In the last speech of King's life, he spoke of all the things he would have missed if he hadn't survived the stabbing 10 years earlier.

The boycott was a good start, but King wanted to reach all of America. In 1958, he wrote a book called *Stride Toward Freedom: The Montgomery Story*. He promoted it on TV and in bookstores. But while he was signing copies in a New York bookstore, a woman stabbed King in the chest. The wound was so close to his heart that any sudden movement, even a sneeze, could have killed him.

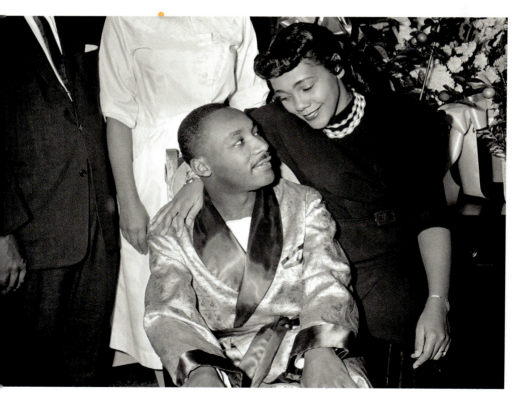

The Kings in Martin's first public appearance after being stabbed, September 1958

While King was recovering, a white woman sent him a letter. "I'm so happy you didn't sneeze," she said.

THE NATIONAL STAGE

By 1960, King devoted all his time to fighting for civil rights. While many Black Americans were angry and wanted to use force to protest unjust laws, King believed the answer was nonviolent resistance.

In a form of protest called sit-ins, some Black students entered "whites only" restaurants. They waited peacefully to be served, even when attacked by customers and arrested by the police.

Lunch Counter Sit-Ins
The first sit-in was at the lunch counter in a Woolworth's department store in Greensboro, North Carolina. It is now a museum dedicated to the civil rights movement.

Ronald Martin, Robert Patterson, and Mark Martin at a whites-only lunch counter in Greensboro, February 1960

Freedom Riders' bus firebombed by the KKK in Anniston, Alabama, May 1961

Civil Rights Movement
In the 1950s and 1960s, Americans fought for equal opportunities and fair treatment for all people regardless of their race. This came to be known as the civil rights movement.

White Allies
Not all white people condoned racist behavior, and many proved it by joining Freedom Rides and marches. Many white allies were viciously attacked for their belief in equality.

Black and white protesters rode from state to state on segregated buses, sharing seats, meals, and risk. White mobs burned buses and beat these "Freedom Riders" with bats and clubs, regardless of their color.

Most Americans were disgusted by the brutality they saw in news coverage of these events. In 1961, the US government outlawed segregation in the interstate transit system.

Church Bombing
As Sunday service was about to begin, white terrorists set off a dynamite bomb at the 16th Street Baptist Church, killing 11-year-old Cynthia Wesley, and 14-year-olds Denise McNair, Carole Robertson, and Addie Mae Collins. Addie's sister Sarah survived but lost her right eye.

In 1963, King moved his focus to Birmingham, Alabama, one of the most segregated cities in the country.

In a series of peaceful marches called the Children's Crusade, hundreds of Black teenagers were arrested. Firefighters blasted them with hoses powerful enough to shred clothing. Police moved in with clubs and dogs trained to attack.

This unprovoked violence outraged people around the world. Feeling the

Black children being blasted with water cannons, Birmingham, May 1963

Jail Time
While behind bars, King wrote his "Letter from Birmingham City Jail," which explained the idea of nonviolent resistance. He encouraged people to break unjust laws without harming others.

KKK
Formed shortly after the Civil War, the Ku Klux Klan is a white-supremacist organization that terrorizes Black Americans. Members wear white hooded robes so no one will recognize them.

pressure, Birmingham city leaders agreed to desegregate businesses and public restrooms and to provide more job opportunities for Black people.

But Birmingham continued to struggle with conflicts around race. In September, the KKK bombed the church where the first Children's Crusade had begun, killing four young girls.

Worker Noble Bradford removing a segregation sign from a bus in Dallas, Texas, April 1956

The 3.5% Rule Researchers have found that whenever at least 3.5 percent of a community dedicates itself to a campaign of nonviolent resistance, it is almost always successful. Nonviolent movements are also twice as likely to reform society as violent uprisings are.

A great wave of support grew for King's method of resistance. "Whites only" notices were torn from the walls of public buildings across America.

> "We know through painful experience that freedom is never voluntarily given by the oppressor, it must be demanded by the oppressed."
>
> —Martin Luther King Jr.

Even the president was paying attention. On June 11, 1963, President John F. Kennedy spoke on national TV, calling for all Americans to be treated equally by both the government and their fellow citizens. He asked Congress to pass a civil rights bill that would make segregation illegal everywhere in the country.

Congress
This branch of government, made up of the Senate and the House of Representatives, creates or abolishes laws. It is made up of people elected from all the US states. Their job is both to speak for their home states and to make decisions about what is best for the whole country.

Emancipation Proclamation

In 1863, while the Civil War was still raging, President Abraham Lincoln declared that all enslaved people living within the states of the Confederacy were free. This was a big step toward abolishing slavery, but it was not the end. Congress officially made slavery illegal after the war, with the 13th Amendment to the Constitution in 1865.

I HAVE A DREAM

1963 marked the 100th anniversary of President Abraham Lincoln's Emancipation Proclamation. King chose that year and the location—the Lincoln Memorial, in the heart of the nation's capital—to share his dream with America. On August 28, a quarter of a million people attended the March on Washington to hear that dream.

"I have a dream!" King said, and his dream was nothing like the nightmare of racism. He dreamed of the day when the descendants of both slaves and slave owners would unite as equals. But before that dream could come true, the country had to make good on its promises of freedom and equality. "Now is the time," he said. Black Americans had been waiting too long already. They would not go back to "business as usual." The applause was tremendous.

Marchers in Washington, D.C., August 28, 1963

Lincoln's Awakening
Lincoln always opposed slavery. Yet he grew up in a time of overwhelming prejudice, and he wasn't sure how many rights free Black people should be given. It took years of soul-searching, and a friendship with the brilliant Black activist Frederick Douglass, for Lincoln to see what equality might look like.

In November of 1963, Kennedy was assassinated. Vice President Lyndon Johnson became president. Many expected the civil rights movement to suffer, since Johnson was a Southerner. But Johnson had been a school teacher in rural Texas, and he knew what poverty and racism could do to a community.

Next in Line
If the president dies or becomes unable to do the job, the vice president becomes president automatically, without a new election. As of 2024, this has happened eight times, four of them following the assassination of the president.

Johnson used all his political skills to get the Civil Rights Act made into law right away. It wouldn't fix all the problems Black people faced, but it was a big step in the right direction. This bundle of laws prevented states and cities from making their own rules to restrict equal rights.

King and Johnson in the Oval Office, December 1963

Civil Rights Act
A hundred years after slavery was abolished in the US, Black people could still be denied basic freedoms, such as equal pay, access to public places, and desegregated schools. In 1964, the government finally made such discrimination illegal with the Civil Rights Act.

33

Black Codes
After the Civil War, southern states passed laws to keep newly freed Black people from becoming equal citizens. People who broke these laws had to pay huge fines, with either money or work. This unpaid labor became a new form of slavery.

By the 1960s, all adult American citizens were allowed by law to vote. Yet many racist laws called "Black codes" still kept Black citizens from actually voting.

In Selma, Alabama, only 335 of 15,000 eligible Black voters were registered to vote. A civil rights organization called the Student Nonviolent Coordinating Committee started a voter education and registration campaign in Selma.

Sheriff Jim Clark ordering King and others to move from a Selma sidewalk where Black people were registering to vote, January 26, 1965

Sheriff Jim Clark telling volunteers from the Selma Voting Rights Campaign to leave the courthouse in Selma, February 1, 1965

King joined the effort. Once again, he was arrested, and once again he wrote from behind bars. He sent a letter to white religious leaders who objected to the protests. He asked why they did not object to police brutality, or racism.

King helped plan a march from Selma to the state capital of Montgomery. Alabama's governor, George Wallace, was determined to prevent it.

Under Suspicion
Many politicians wanted King to stop the protests. The FBI illegally monitored his phone calls, looking for information they could use against him.

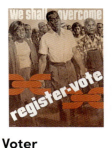

Voter Registration
All Americans who wish to vote must prove their identity, address, and citizenship. This process was meant to be easy, but even today some local and state governments enforce restrictions, attempting to control the outcome of elections.

35

Tear gas fumes in the air, March 7, 1965

Picking a Fight
Civil rights leaders knew it would be pointless to protest in cities where most people agreed with them. They needed America to see racism at its worst, so they only went to cities where racial tensions were high.

The march was planned for March 7, 1965. But after 600 activists crossed Selma's Edmund Pettus Bridge, local and state police attacked them with clubs and tear gas. Police on horseback chased down the fleeing marchers and continued to beat them. They fractured the skull of John Lewis, one of the leaders of the march. The day came to be called "Bloody Sunday."

Two days later, the marchers tried again, this time with twice as many people and led by King. Again, the

Marchers on March 21, 1965.
Front row, left to right: Rosa Parks, Ralph Abernathy, Ruth Harris Bunche, Ralph Bunche, King, Coretta Scott King

36

police were waiting at the other end of the bridge. The marchers knelt and prayed before turning around.

President Johnson called in the army to protect the marchers on their third attempt. The 54-mile trip took five days, and by the time King led the protesters to the capitol steps in Montgomery on March 25, their number had swelled to 25,000.

"We are on the move," King declared, "and no wave of racism can stop us."

Innocent Bystanders? On Bloody Sunday, many people stood by and watched the brutality. Some cheered, others seemed horrified—but they all watched. Such failure to act in the face of injustice or brutality is common today, too. Some places have "duty to rescue" laws that make it illegal to do nothing when others are in danger.

People moving north in 1940

The Great Migration
From 1910 to the 1970s, millions of Black citizens moved out of the Deep South to escape racial violence and the oppressive Jim Crow laws.

Racism was not just a southern problem. In cities such as Detroit and Chicago, many Black people were trapped in poverty, confined to certain neighborhoods. In 1966, King went to Chicago to join the fight for better housing.

But the strategies of nonviolent resistance that had worked so well down south didn't catch on in Chicago. A movement known as Black Power was attracting many young people. They weren't about to let racist citizens and police beat on them without fighting back. During one march, King was struck by a rock. Horrified by the violence, King said, "I have seen many demonstrations in the South but I have never seen anything so hostile and so hateful as I've seen here today."

Home Sweet Home? Even today, unfair policies and racial discrimination make it harder for families of color to find affordable homes in communities where they feel comfortable and safe from harm.

King leading a march in Chicago, August 1966

Vietnam War
Vietnam wanted independence from France, just as Americans had gained independence from England. But instead of a democracy, the North Vietnamese wanted Communism, a form of government that distributes wealth equally, through government control. The US opposed Communism and tried to stop the revolution.

THE OTHER STRUGGLE

By 1965, US troops were fighting in far off Vietnam. Because King was opposed to violence, he and other Christian leaders believed America should stop investing lives and money in war. They thought the US should fix its own problems instead. Muslim leaders like Malcolm X also saw the real enemies as racism and poverty.

American soldiers in Vietnam

40

Top US athletes gathered in support of Muhammad Ali, June 4, 1967

President Johnson agreed with King on civil rights, but not on Vietnam. The more King spoke out against the war, the more Johnson resented it. Many felt that those who didn't support the war were unpatriotic. King would get no more help from the president.

King and Malcolm X, 1964

Resisting War
Many Americans refused to fight in Vietnam. In 1967, Muhammad Ali was banned from boxing for refusing to go. "I have nothing to lose by standing up for my beliefs," he said. "So I'll go to jail. We've been in jail for four hundred years."

Different Dreams
Malcolm X—and the Black Power movement he inspired—didn't trust that equal rights could ever come without force. Nor did he agree with King that the races could, or should, live in the same neighborhoods. His goal was for the races to live in their own communities and leave each other alone.

41

The Kings in Martin's Atlanta office, 1962

Jamaica

Exhausted after years of campaigning, King needed a break. Early in 1967, he visited Jamaica, where he could focus his thoughts. He put them into a new book, *Where Do We Go from Here: Chaos or Community?*

King worried that increased racial tension and the unpopular war in Vietnam could tear America apart. For years, his mission had been to fight segregation, which separated Americans from each other. There had to be a way to bring everyone together. Was there a common problem that oppressed people of every race?

Poverty. That was the problem, and King wanted to work to fix it.

Black and White
In *Where Do We Go from Here?* King noted how the word "black" was often used to describe things that are dirty or bad, while "white" often meant clean, or good. This, he thought, made Black children feel bad about themselves.

Poverty and War
As the war in Vietnam became unpopular, the US started forcing its young men to fight, unless they were in college. Since most poor kids couldn't afford college, the rule was hardly fair.

King began to focus all his attention on the issue of poverty. Good food, jobs, schools, and homes should be available to everyone, he believed. People of all races and backgrounds experienced the misery and hopelessness poverty could bring.

Family in rural Kentucky, 1969

With the Poor People's Campaign, King planned to bring thousands of impoverished people of every race and faith to the nation's capital. They would sleep in tents, close to the White House, until the government promised to improve living conditions nationwide.

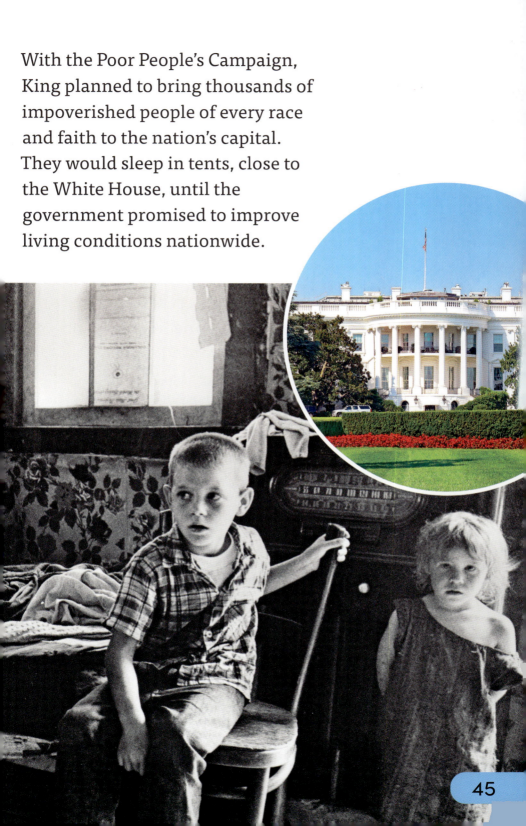

Black Power Salute
At the 1968 Mexico Olympics, two Black American athletes raised clenched fists in gestures of defiance as the US national anthem played. The gesture was meant to show solidarity with oppressed Black people around the world.

MURDER IN MEMPHIS

In 1968, the civil rights spotlight shifted to Memphis, Tennessee. Black sanitation workers had gone on strike, demanding the same pay white workers got. King agreed to help organize a march, but the peaceful protest turned violent when Black Power activists collided with the police. A battle with clubs and guns left one boy dead and many more wounded.

TV news had been showing police attacking peaceful protesters. But now Americans were seeing Black people fighting back. They saw that both sides could initiate violence.

King was devastated. This wasn't the kind of resistance he wanted.

Workers carried these signs to remind people that they deserved equality, dignity, and respect.

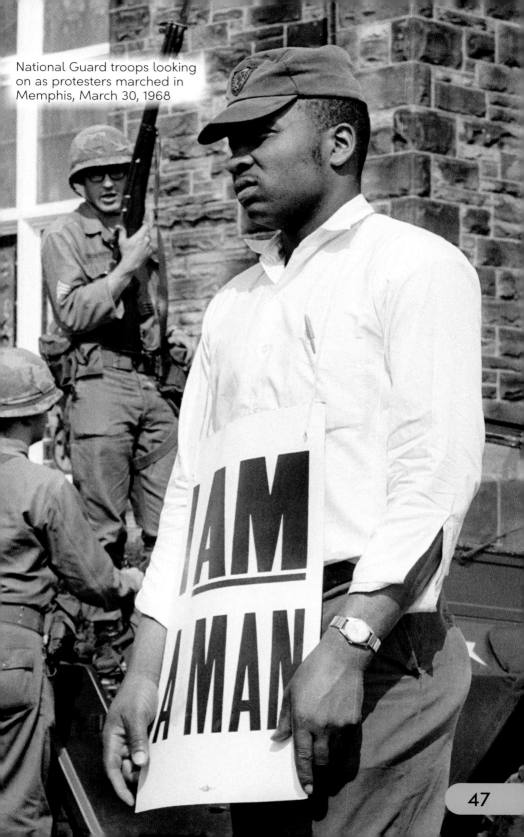

National Guard troops looking on as protesters marched in Memphis, March 30, 1968

King speaking in Memphis on March 18, 1965

King worried that the days of peaceful resistance might be ending. He also sensed the end of his own life. On the evening of April 3, 1968, he spoke to a crowd of thousands, reminding them of how close to death he had come before and admitting how close it seemed now. He didn't want to die. Like everyone else, he wanted a long life. Yet his own life did not matter, he said. God had shown him a brighter future.

"I've seen the Promised Land," he said. "I may not get there with you. But I want you to know tonight, that we, as a people, will get to the Promised Land."

Death was closer for King than anyone thought.

A Better View
King's final speech came to be known as the "Mountaintop" speech, because he used the image of a mountain to symbolize the heights to which he believed God had taken him, to let him see a better future.

Simulated telescopic gunsight showing scene of King's assassination

King spent the next day, April 4, 1968, in his Memphis motel room. That evening, he got dressed for dinner with friends.

But James Earl Ray was waiting for him. After escaping from prison, Ray had tracked King down. Through the scope of his high-powered rifle, he had an excellent view of King's room.

As King stepped onto his balcony, he leaned on the railing to call down to friends in the parking lot. Everyone was happy and making jokes, until a gunshot rang out.

The Lorraine Motel, where King was killed, now the National Civil Rights Museum

Jesse Jackson, King, and Ralph Abernathy on the balcony a day before King's assassination

James Earl Ray
James Earl Ray was a lifelong criminal. His racist beliefs were fueled by the hateful speeches of presidential candidate and Alabama governor George Wallace. For murdering King, Ray spent the rest of his life in prison.

An ambulance rushed him to the hospital, but nothing could be done. The Reverend Dr. Martin Luther King Jr. was dead.

Another Kennedy
Hours after King's assassination, presidential candidate Robert F. Kennedy comforted a largely Black crowd. He reminded them that a white man had killed his brother (President John F. Kennedy) and that violence needed to be replaced by compassion and love. Two months later, Robert Kennedy would also be assassinated.

A POWERFUL LEGACY

King's assassination shocked the world. President Johnson called for a national day of mourning. Thousands attended King's funeral, with millions more watching on TV. Mourners sang the words from his most famous speech: "Free at last, free at last. Thank God Almighty, we are free at last!"

Just a few days later, the Fair Housing Act became law. It prevented housing discrimination based on race, sex, national origin, and religion.

Sanitation workers honoring King as they continued their strike soon after his death, April 1968

A month later, the Poor People's Campaign camped next to the Lincoln Memorial. Demonstrators from all over the country huddled in tents, enduring bad weather and clashes with police. The protest brought real change, including new federal nutrition programs and food assistance for those in need.

A Violent Reaction
Many Black Americans took King's assassination as a sign that white people were not ready for racial equality. Violent riots erupted across 29 states, injuring 3,500 people and killing 39.

> "Oh God, when is this violence going to stop?"
> —Robert Kennedy, hearing that King was dead

Nobel Peace Prize
Alfred Nobel was the inventor of dynamite, a technology he never thought would be used for violence. Its use as a weapon horrified him so much that he created the Nobel Peace Prize, so he would be remembered for peace, not war. Since 1901, this honor has been given each year to the world's most dedicated defender of peace.

King's hard work brought him honor and fame. He was named Man of the Year for 1963 by *Time* magazine. In 1964, he received the Nobel Peace Prize for being the first person in the Western world to show that a struggle can be waged without violence.

Coretta Scott King on the steps of the US Capitol with three of her children, Dexter Scott King (left), Bernice King, and Martin Luther King III, celebrating the enactment of Martin Luther King Jr. Day, November 1983

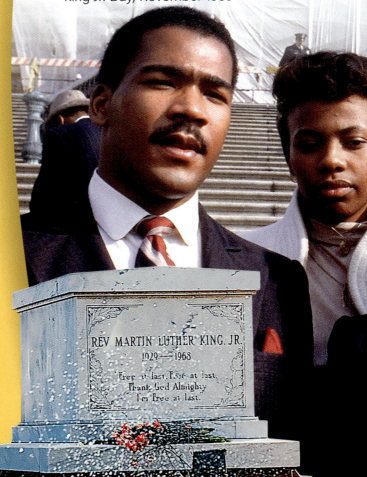

Coretta Scott King helped establish a national holiday to honor her husband's memory, signed into law in 1983. Unlike most holidays, MLK Day comes with a challenge. In 1994, Congress designated it as a national day of service, not leisure—a "day on, not a day off."

Both King's birthplace and grave are national historic sites.

MLK Day
King is the only nonpresident to be honored with a national holiday.

Happy Birthday
Stevie Wonder wrote the song "Happy Birthday" to encourage the government to make King's birthday a holiday.

55

WE SHALL OVERCOME

King achieved nothing alone. He was part of a larger "we," which included many dedicated people with talents and skills different from his. Together, they resisted oppression and shook the conscience of America until it saw what was going on. Here are just a few of the brave people who fought for justice alongside King, and who continued to fight long after he was killed.

Dorothy Height (1912–2010)
Height was already fighting for equality when King was still a boy. A brilliant strategist, she knew how to make things happen, including the 1963 March on Washington.

Ralph Abernathy (1926–1990)
King's best friend, Abernathy marched and prayed with King all through the civil rights movement. After the assassination, he took King's place, continuing to challenge the government's use of tax dollars for wars and space exploration instead of helping underprivileged Americans.

Diane Nash (1938–)
Nash organized sit-ins and Freedom Rides, and continues to fight for voting rights, fair housing, and gender equality. For her lifelong service, she received the Presidential Medal of Freedom in 2022.

John Lewis (1940–2020)
Sit-in organizer, Freedom Rider, and Bloody Sunday survivor John Lewis was beaten and arrested many times for causing what he called "good trouble." He went on to a brilliant career in politics, serving as a congressman for 33 years.

Leading a Vietnam War protest, 1969

CORETTA'S JOURNEY

Coretta Scott King was just as passionate about nonviolence and equality as her famous husband. She took part in many protests, including the march from Selma to Montgomery. She was against the war in Vietnam long before it became unpopular.

Coretta wanted to protect the rights of all who faced discrimination. She wanted the Civil Rights Act of 1964 to include protection for what would eventually be known as the LGBTQ community. She was an early supporter of same-sex marriage.

Speaking at the 25th anniversary of the March on Washington, 1988

At the King Center for Nonviolent Social Change, 1990

In 1985, she was arrested for protesting racial oppression in South Africa. The next year, she met with leaders on both sides of the dispute, Black and white.

Yet of all the causes Mrs. King fought for, none meant more to her than women's rights. If there was one thing men of every color seemed able to agree on, it was keeping women in their place. Even men who fought for civil rights kept women from leadership roles. All through her long life, Mrs. King spoke fearlessly and relentlessly for the rights of women of every color.

> "I don't believe you can stand for freedom for one group of people and deny it to others."
> —Coretta Scott King

Jacqueline Woodson won the author award in 2015.

Coretta Scott King Book Awards Every year, Coretta Scott King Book Awards go to authors and illustrators who create books for children and teens that honestly represent the African American experience.

A NONVIOLENT REVOLUTION

The struggle for equal rights may never end. Yet the civil rights movement dramatically transformed America, making it far more equal, and free, than it was before. Here are just a few events that helped to bring that change.

May 1954: Supreme Court rules school segregation unconstitutional

February 1960: Lunch counter sit-in protests begin

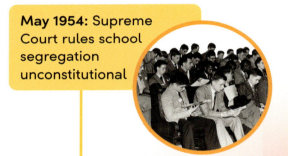

December 1955: Montgomery Bus Boycott begins

May 1961: Freedom Rides begin

May 1968: Poor People's Campaign

May 1963: Children's Crusade marches

July 1964: Civil Rights Act signed into law

August 1963: March on Washington

March 1965: Selma march

61

GLOSSARY

Activist
A person who works to create social change

American Civil War
A war fought in America from 1861 to 1865, between Americans in northern states and Americans in southern states, primarily over the issue of slavery

Assassination
The murder of a well-known person, often for political reasons

Black Power
A movement to gain equality for Black Americans

Civil Rights
Rights that promise equal opportunities and fair treatment for all people regardless of their race, sex, gender, religion, or nationality

Colored
An outdated word for Black people, considered offensive today; it can be used when talking about history or referring to certain organizations

Communism
A form of government that distributes wealth equally, through government control

Conspiracy
A secret plan made by a group

Discrimination
When people are treated unfairly because of their race, religion, or gender

Equality
Treatment that is the same for all people

Federal
Relating to the national government

Freedom Riders
People who rode buses to protest segregation

Injustice
Unfair treatment

Mobilize
To come together or to bring people together in order to take action

Movement
People working together for a cause

Negro
An outdated word for Black people, which can be considered offensive today; it can be used when talking about history

Prejudice
An unreasonable low opinion of something or someone

Protest
To act, speak, or march to change something considered to be wrong

Racism
Unfair treatment because of one's skin color or race

Segregation
Separation of people by their race or skin color

62

INDEX

Abernathy, Ralph 36, 51, 57
Ali, Muhammad 41
assassinations 32, 50–53
Birmingham, Alabama 26–27
Black codes 34
Black Power 39, 41, 46
Bloody Sunday 36, 37, 57
Boycott, Charles 18
Bradford, Noble 28
Bunche, Ralph 36
Bunche, Ruth Harris 36
bus travel
    boycotts 16–19, 21, 60
    Freedom Riders 25, 57, 60
    segregation 12, 28
    "whites before blacks" rule 12, 13, 17
Chicago 38–39
Children's Crusade 26–27, 61
church bombing 26, 27
civil rights movement 24–33, 50, 56–58, 61
Civil War 9, 30
Clark, Jim 34, 35
Collins, Addie Mae 26
Collins, Sarah 26
Communism 40
Congress 29, 30, 57
Constitution 21, 30
Douglass, Frederick 31
Emancipation Proclamation 30
enslaved people 8–9, 30, 31
Freedom Riders 25, 57, 60
Gandhi, Mahatma 15
Great Migration 38
Greensboro, North Carolina 24
Height, Dorothy 56
Hitler, Adolf 11
housing discrimination 38, 39, 52
Jackson, Jesse 51

Johnson, Lyndon 32–33, 37, 41, 52
Kennedy, John F. 29, 32, 52
Kennedy, Robert F. 52, 53
King, Bernice 54
King, Coretta Scott 15–16, 22, 36, 42, 54–55, 58–59
King, Dexter Scott 54
King, Martin Luther, III 54
King, Martin Luther, Jr.
    arrests 20–21, 27, 35
    assassination 50–52
    bus boycott 16–19, 21
    childhood 6–13
    civil rights movement 25–28, 30, 33–39
    college 14
    death threats and attacks on 18, 22–23, 39, 50–51
    honors and awards 54–55
    as minister 14, 16
    name 6–7, 14
    poverty issue 43–45
    speeches 12, 13, 16, 30, 48, 49
    Vietnam War 40–41, 43
    writings 22, 27, 28, 43
King, Martin Luther, Sr. 6–7
KKK (Ku Klux Klan) 25, 27
Lewis, John 36, 57
Lincoln, Abraham 30, 31
Louis, Joe 11
Luther, Martin 7
Malcolm X 40, 41
March on Washington 4, 30–31, 56, 58, 61
Martin, Mark 24
Martin, Ronald 24
Martin Luther King Jr. Day 54, 55
McNair, Denise 26
Memphis, Tennessee 46–51
Montgomery, Alabama 13, 16–19, 21, 35, 37, 58, 60
NAACP 16–17

Nash, Diane 57
Nobel, Alfred 54
Nobel Peace Prize 54
nonviolent resistance 15, 18, 24–28, 39, 46, 49, 58, 60–61
Owens, Jesse 11
Parks, Rosa 17, 36
Patterson, Robert 24
poverty (Poor People's Campaign) 43–45, 53, 61
racism
    attacks on King 18
    Black codes 34
    housing discrimination 38, 39, 52
    Montgomery laws 16
    in northern cities 38–39
    segregation 9–10, 12, 21, 24–28, 60
    "whites before blacks" rule 12, 13, 17
Ray, James Earl 50, 51
riots 53
Robertson, Carole 26
sanitation workers strike 46–49, 52
segregation 9–10, 12, 21, 24–28, 60
Selma, Alabama 34–37, 58, 61
sit-ins 24, 60
slavery 8–9, 30, 31
Student Nonviolent Coordinating Committee 34
Supreme Court 21, 60
Vietnam War 40–41, 43, 44, 58
voting rights 34–35
Wallace, George 35, 51
Washington, D.C. 4, 30–31
Wesley, Cynthia 26
women's rights 59
Wonder, Stevie 55
Woodson, Jacqueline 59

63

QUIZ

Answer the questions to see what you have learned. Check your answers in the key below.

1. Where was Martin Luther King Jr. born?
2. What kind of resistance did King believe was the best way to make change?
3. Which president signed the Civil Rights Act of 1964?
4. Which war did King protest against?
5. What issue was the Poor People's Campaign meant to improve?

1. Atlanta, Georgia 2. Nonviolent resistance 3. Lyndon B. Johnson
4. The Vietnam War 5. Poverty